Blastoff! Beginners are developed by literacy experts and educators to meet the needs of early readers. These engaging informational texts support young children as they begin reading about their world. Through simple language and high frequency words paired with crisp, colorful photos, Blastoff! Beginners launch young readers into the universe of independent reading.

Sight Words in This Book 🔍

a	do	many	some	too
and	eat	of	that	want
are	get	on	them	water
be	have	people	there	with
big	in	play	they	you
can	make	sit	to	

This edition first published in 2021 by Bellwether Media, Inc.

No part of this publication may be reproduced in whole or in part without written permission of the publisher. For information regarding permission, write to Bellwether Media, Inc., Attention: Permissions Department, 6012 Blue Circle Drive, Minnetonka, MN 55343.

Library of Congress Cataloging-in-Publication Data

Names: Leaf, Christina, author.
Title: Birds / by Christina Leaf.
Description: Minneapolis, MN : Bellwether Media, Inc., 2021. | Series: Favorite pets | Includes bibliographical references and index. | Audience: Grades K-1
Identifiers: LCCN 2020007103 (print) | LCCN 2020007104 (ebook) | ISBN 9781644873120 (library binding) | ISBN 9781681037998 (paperback) | ISBN 9781681037752 (ebook)
Subjects: LCSH: Cage birds--Juvenile literature. | Pets--Juvenile literature.
Classification: LCC SF461.35 .L43 2021 (print) | LCC SF461.35 (ebook) | DDC 636.6/8--dc23
LC record available at https://lccn.loc.gov/2020007103
LC ebook record available at https://lccn.loc.gov/2020007104

Text copyright © 2021 by Bellwether Media, Inc. BLASTOFF! BEGINNERS and associated logos are trademarks and/or registered trademarks of Bellwether Media, Inc.

Editor: Amy McDonald   Designer: Jeffrey Kollock

Printed in the United States of America, North Mankato, MN.

Table of Contents

Pet Birds!	4
Care	8
Life with Birds	16
Bird Facts	22
Glossary	23
To Learn More	24
Index	24

Pet Birds!

Do you want a pet that sings? Some birds sing!

There are many kinds of pet birds. They can be colorful.

parakeet

Care

Birds have wide wings. They need big cages.

Cages have **perches**. Birds sit and sleep on perches.

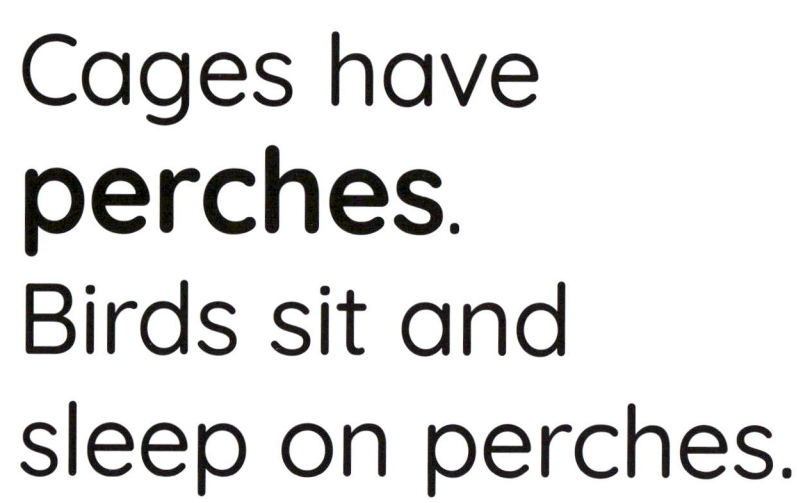

perch

Pet birds eat **pellets**. Seeds are treats!

Birds splash in water dishes. They get clean!

water dish

Life with Birds

Birds love to play! Toys make them happy.

toy

Birds **bond** with people. Some need bird friends, too.

Birds are loud.
Some sing.
Some **whistle**.
Some even talk!

Bird Facts

Pet Bird Supplies

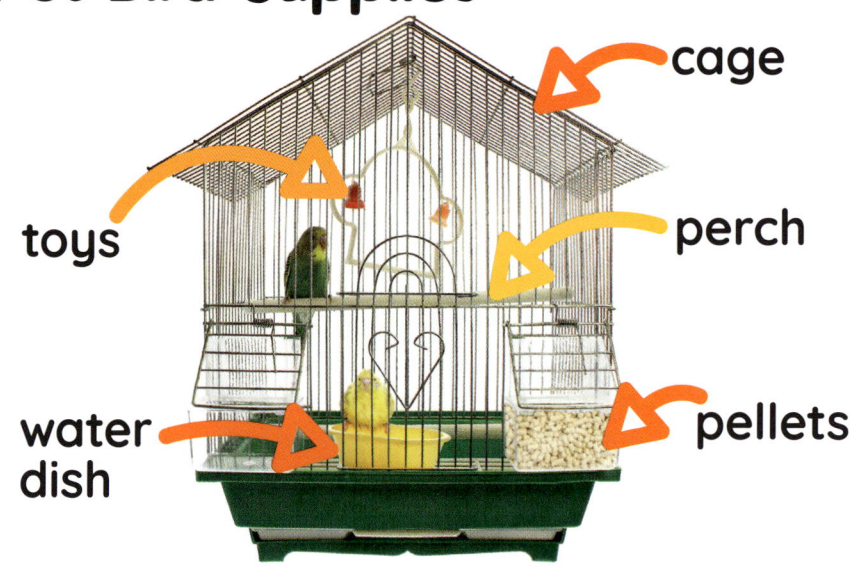

- cage
- toys
- perch
- water dish
- pellets

Bird Toys

puzzles   ropes   swing

Glossary

bond

to become friends

pellets

small pieces of food

perches

spots up high that birds sit on

whistle

to make a sharp, clear sound

To Learn More

ON THE WEB

FACTSURFER

Factsurfer.com gives you a safe, fun way to find more information.

1. Go to www.factsurfer.com.

2. Enter "pet birds" into the search box and click 🔍.

3. Select your book cover to see a list of related content.

Index

bond, 18
cages, 8, 9, 10
clean, 14
color, 6
friends, 18
kinds, 6
pellets, 12
perches, 10
play, 16

seeds, 12, 13
sing, 4, 20
sit, 10
sleep, 10
talk, 20
toys, 16
water dishes, 14
whistle, 20

wings, 8, 9

The images in this book are reproduced through the courtesy of: Tracy Starr, front cover, pp. 7 (hero), 16-17, 18, 22 (puzzles); photomaster, pp. 3, 5; Rosa Jay, p. 4; Denis Tabler, p. 6; cynoclub, p. 7 (cockatiel); Eric Isselee, p. 7 (finch); Thomas Skjaeveland, pp. 8-9; Swat Sirivutcharungchit, p. 10; Edoma, pp. 10-11; Eag1eEyes, p. 12; motorolka, p. 13; VitCOM Photo, p. 14; juniors @ wildlife/ SuperStock, pp. 14-15; Jill Lang, p. 16; Zurijeta, pp. 18-19; Mayskyphoto, pp. 20-21; KonstantinChristian, p. 22 (isolated); Veronika Surovtseva, p. 22 (swing); Juniors Bildarchiv GmbH/ Alamy, p. 22 (ropes); lightofchairat, p. 23 (bond); D. Pimborough, p. 23 (pellets); Poravute Siriphiroon, p. 23 (perches); Jolanta Beinarovica, p. 23 (whistle).